THE VALUE OF BOLDNESS

ILLUSTRATED BY Pileggi

The Story of
Captain Cook

BY ANN DONEGAN JOHNSON

For information write to: ValueTales,
9601 Aero Drive, San Diego, CA 92123

ISBN 0-86679-025-X

This tale is about Captain James Cook,
a man whose bold spirit and thorough knowledge
of seamanship made him one of the greatest
explorers of all time. The story that follows is
based on the events of his life. More historical facts
about James Cook can be found on page 63.

Once upon a time...

many years ago, a boy named James Cook stood at the top of a tall hill in Yorkshire, in the north of England. It was a bright afternoon in late spring, and James had hurried at his task of cleaning out the cow barn so that he could climb Roseberry Topping and still be home in time for supper.

James was a hardworking boy. His father did farm work for a great landowner and James helped him. He also went to the village school because Mr. Scottowe, the landowner, said that he was a bright boy and should have some education. Perhaps he could work in a shop when he was older.

James had never told anybody, but he didn't want to work in a shop. He wanted to go to sea. He dreamed of ocean waves and sailing ships, and every chance he got he climbed this hill and looked eastward as hard as he could. That way lay the sea.

"I see something shining over there," James said to himself. "It must be the sea. Oh, I wish it were closer. I wish I could be like one of those seagulls. Then I'd fly to the sea. I'd fly over the sea and find new places and adventures." He sighed. "But I'll probably spend my whole life right here in the village."

"Why?" said a voice. "Why should you spend your life here if you want to go to sea?"

James looked around. There was no one to be seen. But sitting on a rock not far away was a snow-white seagull. It looked at James with its bright eyes, stretched out its wings and flapped them once or twice as if to fly away. Then it folded them again.

"Aren't you going to answer me?" it said.

"Was that you?" asked James. "I thought I was imagining things."

"Of course it was me," answered the seagull. "I've seen you lots of times, standing up here, staring toward the sea. So, why are you going to spend your life in the village?"

"How could I go to sea?" said James in a discouraged voice. I don't really know much about it, and I don't know anything about sailing or about ships. I don't even know anyone who does."

"You know me, now," said the seagull. "My name is Salty. I don't want to sound conceited, but I probably know as much as anyone about the sea."

"And about ships?" asked James eagerly.

"Well, I've hung around quite a few in my day—but I have to admit I don't know much about how they are run." Seeing how disappointed James looked, Salty added, "That's something you could learn though. Of course, you would have to be bold."

"Bold?" said James.

"Yes," said Salty. "You would have to be bold enough to try something new. No one here can give you the chance you want, so you will have to find it for yourself. And you will have to learn all you can. Being a good seaman takes a lot of knowledge."

"Do you think I could do it?" asked James.

"Of course," said Salty. "If you are bold and work hard."

James looked again to the east and saw that the shadows on the green hill were growing long. "It's getting late!" he exclaimed. "I've got to go."

"So do I," said Salty and he spread his wings, moved them up and down gently and then flapped hard once and rose into the air.

"Will I ever see you again?" called James.

"If you are bold and come to sea." And Salty soared off in the direction of the gleam of the horizon.

"I can't have been talking to a seagull," James told himself as he ran down the steep hill towards home. "It must have been just my own thoughts. I've been thinking so much about going to sea." But he wondered.

He remembered what Salty had said too, and he made up his mind to work as hard as he could at school.

One day the schoolmaster showed the children a map of the world.

"Why are there so many more places marked in Europe than in the rest of the world?" asked James.

"Because there are great parts of the world no one knows much about. Someday bold men will sail over the seas and discover what is out there."

"Maybe when I'm grown up I could go on a voyage like that!"

"If you have any such notions," said the schoolmaster, "you had better get to work on the lesson I set for you this morning. Such sailors will have to be bold *and* know all they can know."

"I've heard that before," thought James, remembering Salty.

One day, when James was seventeen, Mr. Scottowe stopped at the Cooks' cottage. "I've heard of a good opportunity for young James here if he wants to go to work in a shop." James, of course, didn't, but before he could figure out how to say so, Mr. Scottowe continued, "Mr. Sanderson at Staithes is looking for a bright lad."

Staithes! A shop did not sound exciting to James but Staithes did. It was a fishing port and it was on the sea. "Thank you, Mr. Scottowe," he stammered, adding to himself, "maybe in Staithes I'll find my chance to go to sea. Maybe I'll even see Salty."

James worked hard for Mr. Sanderson, measuring yard
goods, weighing flour, sweeping out the shop. Whenever he
could get away he went down to the sea front and watched
the fishing boats sailing in and out. He watched the seagulls
too.

One day when he had been in Staithes for about a year, he was watching the boats and dreaming of going to sea in one of them when he heard a familiar voice.

"I've been waiting for you to come to sea," it said. "What's taking you so long?"

James turned and there was Salty, sitting on a rock.

"Oh, Salty," said James, "I still want to be a sailor. But how can I? I work in a shop."

"That doesn't mean you have to stay there forever," said Salty. "Have you told anyone that what you really want is a ship, not a shop? As I said before, you have to be bold or you'll never get a chance to do what you want."

James knew Salty was right. "I haven't . . . but I will.
Mr. Sanderson knows lots of people. Maybe he would help me
if he knew how much I want to go to sea. I'll go tell him right
now!" And he did.

"Well, James," said the kindly Mr. Sanderson, "you're a good
lad but I had an idea you had something on your mind. So
you want to be a sailor. Now me, I'm happy safe on land.
But we need bold fellows like you too. I'll talk to my friend
John Walker. He's a ship owner down at Whitby."

And so it was that James Cook became a sailor.

For eight years he worked for John Walker and other owners on
ships that carried coal up and down the east coast of England
and up to Scandinavia and into the Baltic Sea. He learned much
about navigating in dangerous waters and about handling ships
in all weather.

During the winters, when the ships were laid up for refitting,
James studied mathematics and anything else he thought
might be useful.

One day, while his ship was being unloaded in the port of London, James was sitting at the end of a dock staring at the Thames River when Salty swooped down and perched on a piling beside him.

"You've done well," said Salty. "I've watched you up and down the coast and I'd say you've learned a lot about sailing. I guess Mr. Walker thinks so too, since he made you mate of the *Friendship*."

"That's not all," said James. "Now he wants to make me captain."

"That's great," said Salty. "But then why are you sitting out here alone, looking so serious?"

"I am not sure I want to stay in the coal trade. I want to see more of the world and learn new things. Actually, I am thinking of joining the Navy."

"The Navy!" exclaimed Salty. "Now that *would* be a bold step. It's a hard life, though, and you would have to start again as a common sailor."

"I know," said James. "But with the trouble between England and France, the Navy is expanding. I think I'd advance fast."

"You might at that," said Salty. "I told you to be bold and you are certainly taking my advice."

James joined the Navy and he did advance quickly. In two years, he had qualified to be master of one of His Majesty's ships. As master he was responsible for the navigation and management of the ship, subject only to orders from the captain.

Soon James was sailing for North America as master of the *Pembroke*. He was glad to see Salty among the seagulls that followed the ship.

"You'll have to be bold, where you're going," Salty said to James one day. "I hear France and England are at war."

"Yes, I am afraid so," said James. "It looks as though the fleet will be ordered to go up the St. Lawrence River to support the army at Quebec." And that is, indeed, what happened.

When the ships had travelled a fair way up the river, the captain spoke to James. "There are two hundred ships here waiting to sail the rest of the way to Quebec. But the river is very treacherous at this point and our scouts tell us that the buoys that mark the safe channel have been removed."

"In that case, sir," said James, "we'll just have to re-chart and re-buoy the river."

"Take the men and the boats you need," said the captain.

For several weeks James Cook and his men worked, mostly at night and sometimes under fire. Finally, the job was done and every ship in the British fleet sailed safely through one of the most dangerous stretches of river in the world.

The charts that James Cook made during those weeks continued to be used for over a hundred years.

Early one morning when James came up on deck to inspect the men on watch he found Salty sitting on the rail.

"You've been up to all sorts of new things since I saw you last," his friend remarked.

"I've learned a lot," said James. "I've been studying astronomy and I met a fellow who has been teaching me surveying. But none of that seems very bold to me."

"There's more than one way to be bold," said Salty. "Carrying on your work under dangerous conditions is one. And another is bothering to learn things no one would expect you to. You never know where your knowledge will lead you."

"Maybe so," replied James. "But what I need now are new places to chart and something new to see in the sky."

James was soon to get the first of his wishes. He was given command of a ship and appointed to chart the coast of Newfoundland. For the next five years, he spent his summers surveying and charting, and his winters in England getting his charts ready for publication.

During one of his stays in England, James met a pretty young woman named Elizabeth Batts. So far, James had always been too busy with his studies and his life and work at sea to think much about a home and family. Elizabeth, with her sparkling dark eyes, changed all that.

"I want to marry her, Salty," he told his friend one day. "But I can't give up the sea, and that means I'd be away for months on end. What hope is there that she would have me under those conditions?"

"None at all if you don't ask her," answered Salty bluntly. "As I keep telling you ..."

"I know what you're going to say: 'Be bold!' And you're right. I'll ask her tonight."

As it turned out, Elizabeth was just as much in love as James—
and just as bold in her own way. She said "yes" without the least
hesitation, and so the two were married.

James bought a house near London in a village called Mile End,
and soon he had a baby son to come home to as well as a wife.

In the midst of all these exciting events, James did not lose his interest in astronomy. In 1766 he observed an eclipse of the sun and sent a report of his observations to the Royal Society, an organization devoted to scientific research.

"There's something even more exciting than an eclipse coming up in three years," James told Salty one day. "The planet Venus is going to pass between the earth and the sun. But it will only be possible to observe it properly from the South Pacific, so I'll miss it."

"Are you sure?" said Salty. "Three years ago did you think you would be doing any astronomical observations at all? Remember, be bold! You never know what might happen."

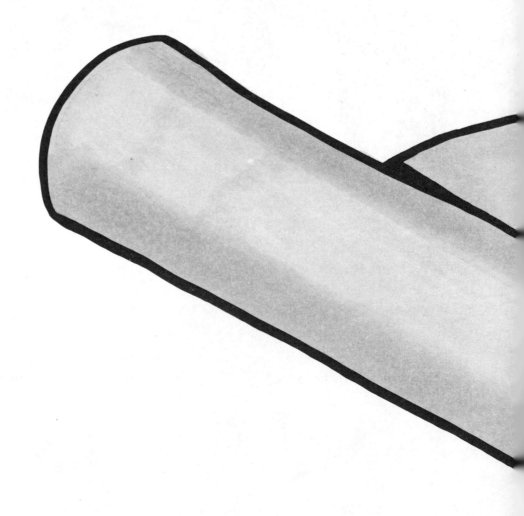

In fact, the Royal Society was planning to send an expedition to Tahiti to observe the Transit of Venus, as it was called. The expedition would also explore the South Pacific to look for a great southern continent which many people believed must exist.

To command the expedition, the Society needed a bold and experienced seaman who could manage a ship in all kinds of weather and sail wisely in uncharted waters; one who could make maps of any new lands that were discovered and who was a capable astronomer as well.

Who do you think they chose?

Of course. They chose the one man who was all these things: James Cook!

"I told you all that studying would lead you into adventure," said Salty as James readied his ship, the *Endeavour*, for the voyage. "Now you'll really have to be bold. Even I don't know much about the Pacific."

"I'm going to have plenty of help on this adventure," said James. "The Royal Society is sending men who know all about plants and animals. There's an astronomer and an artist to draw the things we find. And a doctor. And a goat. We'll even have fresh milk."

"I'm glad I'll be flying," said Salty. "It sounds crowded." The *Endeavour* was crowded, but James felt comfortable with her because she was one of the strong, wide coal ships he had first sailed in out of Whitby. He knew she was a tough little ship, not fast but very sea-worthy.

The voyage across the Atlantic and down the east coast of South America went smoothly. The scientists went ashore as often as possible to collect new varieties of animals and plants. At sea they caught many ocean creatures and kept busy studying, drawing and preserving what they had collected.

One day the mate came to James. "The men are complaining about the food, sir," he said. "They don't want to eat the sauerkraut."

"Well, they have to," said James. "I've seen how men sicken with scurvy on long voyages. I believe it's because they have no fresh fruit or vegetables. Sauerkraut is a good substitute and one we can carry."

The mate shook his head. "I'm afraid the only way to get them to eat it will be to punish them if they don't."

"If I have to I will," replied James. "But maybe there's another way. We'll give them a few days. Meanwhile, every officer is to demand a second helping of sauerkraut at every meal and eat it with great enthusiasm."

"Every officer, sir?" asked the mate weakly.

"Every officer," said James. And remember, *great* enthusiasm."

The trick worked. Soon the men were eating so much sauerkraut James had to ration it.

In January 1769 James Cook took the *Endeavour* into an inlet in the island called Tierra del Fuego at the very tip of South America.

"Soon we'll be around Cape Horn," he said to Zachary Hicks, his second in command. The voyage has gone so well that I will call this place the Bay of Good Success. Perhaps that will bring us success on the rest of the voyage."

But James knew that rounding Cape Horn was risky. Often huge waves and fierce winds greeted ships in those waters. He hesitated in the calm inlet before sailing out into the open sea.

"You'll have to be bold, James, and sail the best you can," said Salty. "There's nothing you can do about the weather."

But James and the *Endeavour* had good luck with the weather. Calm seas allowed the ship to go slowly so that James could chart those dangerous waters.

Eight months after leaving England, the *Endeavour* arrived in Tahiti. Not only was the ship in good order, but not one of the crew was on the sick list. The sailors were, however, getting rather tired of sauerkraut by now and were glad there were fresh fruits and vegetables to be had from the Tahitians.

The expedition stayed in Tahiti for about three months. James and the astronomer from the Royal Society observed the Transit of Venus, the other scientists collected many specimens and everyone enjoyed the beautiful islands. When the time came to move on, no one wanted to leave and the Tahitians, who had become friendly with the Englishmen, did not want them to go. The night before they were due to sail, James spoke quietly with Zachary.

"The men have been happy here, I know," he said. "Do you think many of them will try to desert?"

"No, I don't think so, sir," answered Zachary. "They are devoted to you. However much they might like to stay, they will go when you say the word."

"I hope you're right, because we must carry on with the rest of our voyage. There may be a great continent to explore and certainly there will be many islands to chart."

Zachary was right, and the next morning the *Endeavour* sailed on into unknown seas. One of the native chiefs, a man named Tupia, sailed with them.

"I know much about the islands to the west and the south," he said. "I can talk the languages of the people who live there. I can help you."

"Do you think there is a great continent to the south?" asked James.

"My father was a greater traveler than I. He went far to the south and he saw only islands."

"We must try to find out for sure," said James.

They sailed for nearly 1500 miles to the south and found no land. The weather was terrible. Both ship and sails had to be repaired constantly and the crew was exhausted.

One day James found Salty perched on deck in the shelter of the cabin. "What now, Salty?" he asked his friend. "We sail and sail and we find nothing."

"If you find nothing to the south, you must boldly change direction," answered Salty.

So James turned the *Endeavour* toward the west. Early one morning three long weeks later, there came an excited cry from the mast-head.

"Land ho!"

They had reached New Zealand. James named the promontory that had been sighted Young Nick's Head after the young sailor who had first seen it.

New Zealand had been discovered 126 years before. No European had seen it since, and no one had ever tried to sail around it. James Cook set out to discover whether it was an island or part of a larger continent.

As the *Endeavour* sailed up the east coast toward the northern tip of New Zealand, the wind blew more and more fiercely against the little ship. James thought of putting into a sheltered inlet and waiting for calmer seas.

As he stood looking at the waves breaking over the bow of his ship he was sure he saw Salty riding the wind with his wings outstretched.

"Be bold!" his friend seemed to be calling over the roar of the wind. "If you wait you may never do it!"

Two weeks later, on Christmas day, the *Endeavour* rounded the top of New Zealand and went on to sail around both the North and South Islands. James Cook had proved that New Zealand was not part of a larger continent. He had also charted the coast and given names to hundreds of bays, peaks, rivers and inlets. Many of those names are still used today.

"We have completed our work," James said to his officers. "We can return home. Or we can be the first to explore the east coast of Australia. What do you say?"

The officers knew perfectly well what James wanted to do. They had been away for a long time, but not one of them hesitated.

"Of course we must sail on," said Zachary Hicks. "Home will still be there a few months from now," said the mate, "but who knows if we'll ever be here again?"

Inspired by James Cook's bold spirit, all the officers had come to feel that no chance of new discoveries was to be missed. The weather was good as they sailed up the coast of Australia. There were many bays and islands to chart and name. The scientists gathered hundreds of new plants and animals. Near one bay they found so many new plants that James named it Botany Bay.

Then, one night, there was a terrible crunch and a shock that shook the *Endeavour* from stem to stern. The ship had grounded on a coral reef. She was stuck fast and water was pouring in a large hole. The crew manned the pumps but water still came in. The situation was desperate. Shore was more than twenty miles away and there weren't enough boats to carry everyone to safety.

James had to make a bold plan. He had the men throw overboard as much material as could be spared. Then he had them arrange the anchors so that the ropes could be used to pull the ship off the reef during high tide.

While they waited for the tide to rise, Salty came and perched
on the railing. "You're in a tight spot this time," he said. "You'll
need courage to go through with that bold plan. There will be a
hole in the ship when you get her clear."

"I know," said James. "But if she floats we'll be all right. "And
the *Endeavour* did float. A piece of coral had broken off and
partly plugged the huge hole. James ordered the men to further
plug it with a sail tied under the bottom of the ship.

"What if the ship can't be repaired?" asked a mate as they slowly
sailed for the coast.

"We'll take her apart and use the timbers to build a smaller
ship," answered James.

But the skillful ship's carpenters and blacksmiths were able to mend the gash, and a few weeks later, the *Endeavour* started the long journey home.

Unfortunately, it became necessary to stop at Batavia, in the East Indies, for more thorough repairs to the ship. Batavia was an unhealthy port, full of tropical diseases. Many of the crew who had been healthy for the whole voyage now became ill and some died.

"It's a sad way to start the journey home," James said to Salty as the ship sailed out of Batavia harbor.

"Still, when you get there, you will have something to tell people about how to prevent scurvy," said Salty.

"Will they listen to me? I'm only a sailor."

"They will if you tell them boldly exactly what you did and how they can do the same."

"I'll tell them," vowed James Cook.

Two years and eleven months after leaving England the *Endeavour* sailed into her home port. James was delighted to find that Elizabeth and their two sons had come from Mile End to meet him. James had sent letters whenever he could, and now young James, who was nearly eight, and six-year-old Nathaniel were full of questions about their father's adventures.

"Weren't you scared when all that water was coming in the ship?"

"How do you make friends with people when you don't talk the same language?"

"Tell me some more about the time…"

"Can I be a sailor like you when I grow up?"

James laughed and answered all their questions. When he came to the last, he grew more serious. "A long time ago, when I was not much older than you, James, a good friend told me what to do if I wanted to go to sea. 'Be bold,' he said, 'and learn everything you can.' It was good advice. If you follow it then, yes, you can probably be a sailor like me some day."

Many other people were waiting to hear all about the expedition too. The Royal Society, the Royal Navy and the public were thrilled with all the discoveries. Those who understood seamanship regarded James Cook as the greatest explorer and navigator of the time.

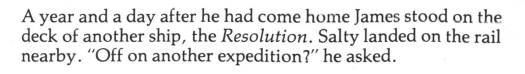

A year and a day after he had come home James stood on the deck of another ship, the *Resolution*. Salty landed on the rail nearby. "Off on another expedition?" he asked.

"Yes," said James. "Some people still think there must be a big continent to the south. We're going to look for it."

"Do you really think there is such a thing?"

"It doesn't matter, I'm looking for whatever I can find. I want to go as far south as I can sail the ship."

"That will take all your bold spirit. Mine too. Those aren't what you would call friendly seas." And Salty flapped his wings and rose into the air.

Salty was right. Sailing that far south meant sailing into dangerous ice-filled seas. For months the ropes and sails were stiff with ice. For months the sailors endured freezing winds outside and damp cold in the cabins. For months James spent most of his time on deck making sure his ship did not sail too close to the towering icebergs.

By the end of the voyage, the *Resolution* had sailed south of the Antarctic Circle in three different oceans—the Pacific, the Atlantic and the Indian Ocean. In fact, James Cook and his crew were the first people to sail around the world so far to the south.

Because of pack ice that covered the surface of the ocean near Antarctica, the *Resolution* never reached that southernmost continent. But James Cook proved that any body of land so far to the south was both small and uninhabitable.

Not all of the three-year-long voyage was spent in cold oceans so far to the south. James visited Tahiti twice and was welcomed gladly by the Tahitians. He revisited New Zealand and discovered many new islands, including a group he called the Friendly Islands because the people there were so friendly.

One day Salty perched on the rail near James and said, "This has been a bold voyage for sure. You have sailed the Pacific Ocean up and down and back and forth. There isn't much left to discover in the southern hemisphere."

"I guess that means it's time to go home," said James.

A lot happened to James back in England. Because of his contributions to science, he was made a Fellow of the Royal Society. He was given a gold medal for his work in keeping sailors healthy at sea. He was given the official rank of Captain and a comfortable job for the Navy with good pay and no danger.

But James was not really happy being safe and comfortable. He had told Salty once that he could not give up the sea, and it was still true.

"They have honored me so much," he complained to his friend one day, "I'm afraid they've forgotten I want to be a plain ship's captain, sailing the seas."

"I don't think you'll spend the rest of your life on land," said Salty reassuringly. "Remember, if you're bold and take a chance when it comes to you, you'll have adventures. It happened to you before. It will happen again."

One day the Lords of the Admiralty invited James to a grand dinner. They began talking about sending an expedition to find the Northwest Passage.

"If only we could find a way around the top of North America," said one man.

"People have been searching for it for three hundred years," said another, "but with the right man in command the expedition might well succeed."

"We're ready to supply ships and all that is needed," said a third, "but everything depends on finding a fine seaman and experienced explorer to take charge."

James looked around the table. "My lords," he said, "I would be happy to command this expedition if you would allow me to."

The Lords of the Admiralty smiled. This was just what they had hoped for.

The plan was for James to take two ships, the *Resolution* and the *Discovery*, up the west coast of North America, find a passage around the north and meet another ship coming from the east.

The first part of the trip went so well that James was able to spend some time in Tahiti and other South Pacific islands, places he loved. Then the two ships sailed north.

When Salty floated in one evening on a warm breeze, James was glad to see him. "I know the South Pacific so well by now," he said. "It feels good to be heading into unknown waters again."

"You'll always find something new to explore if you are bold enough to keep trying," said Salty.

"I'll keep trying," said James.

Soon they reached a beautiful group of islands which James named the Sandwich Islands, after the Earl of Sandwich. They are now called the Hawaiian Islands. The people greeted him warmly and James hoped he would be able to return. But now he had to hurry north.

Once the ships reached the coast of North America, strong
winds made the passage northward very difficult. About two-
thirds of the way up Vancouver Island they had to stop for four
weeks for repairs. The Nootka Indians who lived there were
peaceable and friendly, and the country was beautiful. Still
James was glad when the northward voyage could begin again.
The two ships continued around the Alaskan Peninsula and into
an arm of the Arctic Ocean. Then suddenly the weather
worsened and they were faced with ice that stretched from
horizon to horizon. For a week James searched for a way
through. Then he called his officers together.

"If we stay, we may get frozen in," he said. "We will return to the Sandwich Islands, winter there, and try again next summer."

We know now that there is always ice in the Arctic Ocean, blocking the way of any ordinary ship. But James Cook never knew this for he never came back to North America.

He took his ships back to the Sandwich Islands as he had planned. The natives were delighted to see him and all went well for a time. Then a dispute broke out between the crew and some natives over a stolen boat. When James Cook tried to end the dispute he was killed in a brief fight.

His crew mourned him deeply for they both respected his seamanship and loved him as a captain who truly cared for the welfare of his men.

Because of his thorough knowledge of seamanship and his bold spirit, James Cook became one of the greatest navigators and explorers the world has ever known.

Now, you probably don't dream of going to sea or making great discoveries as James Cook did when he was young. You have your own dream, and that is how it should be.

But, whatever your dream is, you will stand a better chance of making it come true if, like James Cook, you face life with a bold spirit—if you are always ready to study and learn new things, to try a different way, to seek out opportunities instead of waiting for them to come to you.

And if you do that, whether your dream really comes true or not, you will live a fuller, more exciting and happier life.

The End

James Cook was born in Marton, England, on October 27, 1723. His father was a farm laborer. James was a bright lad and his father's employer helped him to attend the village school.

When he was 17 James went to work in a grocer and dry goods shop in Staithes, a fishing village about twelve miles from his home. Within two years he left Staithes and apprenticed himself to John Walker, a Quaker ship owner at Whitby, an important port farther south on the Yorkshire coast.

For eight years James worked on the coal ships that plied up and down the British coast and sailed to Scandinavia and the Baltic ports. These sturdy vessels gave James excellent training in practical seamanship. During the winters he also studied mathematics and any other subject he thought would help him advance.

In 1755 James was offered the command of one of Mr. Walker's ships but he chose instead to join the Royal Navy. In those days life in the Navy was very hard and James had to go back to being a common seaman. However, war between England and France was just beginning and James may have guessed that the Navy would be expanding quickly and there would be plenty of chance for advancement.

In May of 1759 James sailed for North America as Master of the *Mercury*. During the years he spent in what is now Canada, James Cook took part in the charting of the St. Lawrence River which allowed the British fleet to reach Quebec safely. He learned surveying and studied astronomical navigation and more mathematics. His superior officers were very much impressed by his industry and ability, and he was given the job of surveying and charting the coast of Newfoundland.

In fact, the charts that James made during this time would be used for more than a century. James quickly gained a reputation for being an excellent navigator and chart-maker. He also observed an eclipse of the sun and sent his observations to the Royal Society.

During the years that James spent in North America he returned several times to England. In 1762 he married Elizabeth Batts and by 1764 he had two sons, James and Nathaniel. In 1768 the Royal Society decided to send an expedition to Tahiti to observe the Transit of Venus, that is the passage of the planet Venus between the earth and the sun. The expedition was also to do extensive exploring in the South Pacific and to look for a great continent which many people thought existed there.

James Cook was chosen to lead this expedition. Accompanying him were scientists and artists who were to study and record new animals, plants and places. The expedition was a great success. The Transit of Venus was observed, New Zealand was circumnavigated and charted, the east coast of Australia was explored, and many new islands were discovered.

After James and his ship, the *Endeavour*, returned to England in 1771 a new expedition under his command was planned almost at once. The

JAMES COOK
1723-1779

Resolution and the *Adventure* were simply to explore the South Pacific and, if possible to discover whether the great southern continent did exist.

This second voyage was one of the great journeys of exploration in the history of the world. James's ship the *Resolution* sailed farther south than any ship had ever sailed and proved that there could be no large continent to the south. In addition many islands were discovered and charted. By the time James returned to England the map of the southern Pacific was nearly as complete as it is today.

When an expedition to look for a northwest passage around the top of North America was planned, James Cook volunteered to command it. His offer was eagerly accepted. This expedition gave James a chance to visit again the islands of Tahiti, which he loved, and on his way north he discovered the Hawaiian Islands. The passage up the coast of Canada was difficult and both ships had to be repaired part-way up Vancouver Island. They sailed as far north as the Bering Strait but had to turn back because of pack ice. James planned to spend the winter in the Hawaiian Islands and return to the north in the summer. He had generally gotten on very well with native peoples and he expected no trouble. However, something went wrong and in a scuffle over a stolen boat, James Cook was killed, on February 14, 1779.

James Cook was mourned by his crew because he was a fair and honest captain as well as a fine seaman. Sailors everywhere owed him a debt because he realized and told others how important fresh food and clean quarters were to the health of a crew. He set new standards in navigation and map-making as well as in the care of the men under his command. Maps of the Pacific still show hundreds of names which he gave to islands, peaks, bays and rivers. James Cook was truly one of the great sailors and explorers of all time.

The ValueTale Series